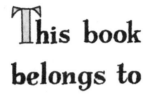

This book belongs to

Nicholas Marco

The BIBLE PROMISE BOOK FOR PRESCHOOLERS

Written and Illustrated by
Kathy Arbuckle

A Barbour Book

Member of the Evangelical Christian Publishers Association

Published by Barbour & Company, Inc.
P.O. Box 719
Uhrichsville, Ohio 44683

Printed in Hong Kong.

Thy Word is a lamp unto my feet, and a light unto my path.

PSALM 119:105

Contents

Being Me

I Love My Family–*parents' duties* *8*

I Am Happy–*contentment, joy,*
   obedience, praise *12*

I Am Strong–*courage* *20*

I Have Jobs–*laziness* *24*

I Tell the Truth–*honesty* *26*

I Get Mad–*anger* *30*

I Am Scared–*fear, peace, protection,*
   enemies, help *32*

I Am Sorry–*forgiveness, repentance* *38*

I Really Am Rich–*money, sharing* *46*

I Get Sick–*sickness* *50*

I Want to be Smart–*wisdom* *52*

Knowing God

God Is Love—*loving God, God's love,*
righteousness, loving each other *54*

God Is Your Best Friend—*about God* *64*

God Gives You Good Things—*food*
and clothing *66*

God Helps You Grow—*fruitfulness* *70*

God Is There—*seeking God, trust* *72*

God Is Like a Map—*guidance* *78*

God Has a Book—*God's Word* *80*

God Wants You to Pray—*prayer* *84*

God Has a Home—*eternal life, salvation* *90*

The Bible Promise Book for Preschoolers

Children, obey your parents in all things: for this is well pleasing unto the Lord.

COLOSSIANS 3:20

Do your parents tell you to do things?

Your mommy and daddy love you very much. They always want what is best for you. That's why they tell you what to do. Did you know that God put you and your parents together? God wants you to do what Mommy and Daddy say to do. God always knows what is best for you.

The Bible Promise Book for Preschoolers

Train up a child in the way he should go: and when he is old, he will not depart from it.

PROVERBS 22:6

Do your parents talk to you about God?

Your mommy and daddy want you to know about God. They want you to know how much God loves you. Someday you and your parents will live together with God in heaven.

The Bible Promise Book for Preschoolers

But godliness with contentment is great gain.

I TIMOTHY 6:6

Do you have everything you want?

What you want and what you need are two different things. You may want lots of toys that you don't have. But God knows what you need. God has given you family, friends, sunshine and rain, food, clothes, and especially love. That's all you really need to be happy.

My lips shall greatly rejoice when I sing unto Thee.

PSALM 71:23

Do you like to sing?

We can tell God how happy He makes us by singing happy songs to Him. He loves to hear you sing. Your songs show God how much you love Him.

The Bible Promise Book for Preschoolers

And thou shalt do that which is right and good in the sight of the Lord: that it may be well with thee. DEUTERONOMY 6:18

Do you think about God?

In the Bible, God's special Book, God tells how He wants you to live. When you live as God wants, you will be happy. When you live as God wants, God will show you how happy He is. He will always take care of you.

I will bless the Lord at all times: His praise shall continually be in my mouth.

PSALM 34:1

What has God given you today?

You have so many reasons to say thank you to God. Just think... God gives you a night of sleep and a day of sunshine. He gives you a friend to laugh with, a dog to hug, and a mommy or daddy to listen. Thank God every day for all He has given you. God wants you to be happy!

The Bible Promise Book for Preschoolers

Be of good courage, and
He shall strengthen your
heart, all ye that hope in
the Lord.

PSALM 31:24

Can God make you strong?

God made the whole universe and
everything that is in it. God knows
everything, too. If you love God, God
will make you strong and brave.

The Lord is my helper, and I will not fear what man shall do unto me.

HEBREWS 13:6

Do you know someone who picks on you?

Almost everybody has known a bully. God says that we should love bullies. We should even pray for them! Ask God to help you. With God as your helper, you can face anyone and not be afraid.

The Bible Promise Book for Preschoolers

He that tilleth his land shall have plenty of bread.

PROVERBS 28:19

Do you have jobs to do at home?

Do you have to make your bed or put your toys away? Everyone has jobs to do. God says that if we do our jobs, we will make our families happy. God is happy when He sees you helping your parents and others.

The Bible Promise Book for Preschoolers

Ye shall not steal, neither deal falsely, neither lie one to another.

LEVITICUS 19:11

Have you ever told a lie?

Even though you don't want to get in trouble, telling a lie is a bad idea. God's Son Jesus said He is the way, the truth, and the life. Like Jesus, you should always tell the truth.

The Bible Promise Book for Preschoolers

Lying lips are abomination to the Lord: but they that deal truly are His delight.

PROVERBS 12:22

Do lies make God happy?

The Bible says God hates lies. When you tell a lie you hurt yourself and others. God knows when you lie and when you tell the truth. The truth makes God happy.

The Bible Promise Book for Preschoolers

A soft answer turneth away wrath: but grievous words stir up anger.

PROVERBS 15:1

Do you get mad sometimes?

Sometimes someone or something can make you very mad. God wants you to be like His Son, Jesus. Jesus said you should be nice to each other. You should use kind words.

The Bible Promise Book for Preschoolers

For I the Lord thy God will hold thy right hand, saying unto thee, Fear not; I will help thee. ISAIAH 41:13

Why does your daddy or mommy hold your hand when you cross the street?

Your parents want to keep you safe. Sometimes things around you can be scary. God knows this, too. He doesn't want you to be afraid. God is with you – and your daddy and mommy – to help you be careful.

The Bible Promise Book for Preschoolers

And the peace of God, which passeth all understanding, shall keep your hearts and minds through Christ Jesus.

PHILIPPIANS 4:7

Do you ever wonder what will happen next?

Maybe you feel scared when you see pictures of wars. Or maybe someone you love is sick and you wonder if they'll ever get better. God is in control of the whole world. In fact, the whole universe! Can you imagine how big God is? God is able to take away every scary thought. God is able to do anything.

I will both lay me down in peace, and sleep: for Thou, Lord, only makest me dwell in safety. PSALM 4:8

Are you ever afraid of the dark?

Many people are scared of things they can't see. But God is with you all the time. Every single minute and second of the day and night God is there. Wherever you go, you are not alone. You don't have to be scared of the dark anymore.

The Bible Promise Book for Preschoolers

The Lord is gracious, and full of compassion; slow to anger, and of great mercy.

PSALM 145:8

How do you feel when you do something bad?

God loves you very much. But He feels sad when He sees you do something bad. Tell Him how sorry you are. Ask Him to help you do the right thing next time.

I Am Sorry

The Bible Promise Book for Preschoolers

And be ye kind one to another, tenderhearted, forgiving one another, even as God for Christ's sake hath forgiven you. EPHESIANS 4:32

What does it mean to forgive?

If someone does something bad to you, and they say they are sorry, you forgive them if you say, "That's okay." Jesus said you should forgive others seventy times seven. (Let's see. That would be 490 times.) That is a lot of forgiving, but that is what God wants you to do.

If we confess our sins, He is faithful and just to forgive us our sins.

I JOHN 1:9

How does God forgive you?

The second you tell God you are sorry, God forgives you. God says, "That's okay." You should also tell God that you will try very hard never to do that bad thing again. God is your Heavenly Father. He wants you to learn from your mistakes.

He that covereth his sins shall not prosper: but whoso confesseth and forsaketh them shall have mercy.

PROVERBS 28:13

When you do something wrong, do you try to pretend you haven't?

God always knows the truth. He sees everything you do. Don't blame someone else for your actions or tell a lie. Tell God you are sorry. God will forgive you.

The Bible Promise Book for Preschoolers

A little that a righteous man hath is better than the riches of many wicked.

PSALM 37:16

Will lots of money make you happy?

Only for a little while. No matter how much money you have, you will never have enough to buy everything you want. And if money is all you want, you won't be happy. Only God can give you real happiness. You are really rich if you know God loves you and you love God.

I Really Am Rich

The Bible Promise Book for Preschoolers

Inasmuch as ye have done it unto one of the least of these my brethren, ye have done it unto Me.

MATTHEW 25:40

Do you like to give presents?

You don't have to be rich to give a present to someone. Sharing whatever you might have can make someone happy. You could give a present of your time or something special you made all by yourself. You could give a toy you don't play with anymore. Whenever you share with others, you are sharing with Jesus.

The Bible Promise Book for Preschoolers

For I will restore
health unto thee, and I
will heal thee of thy
wounds, saith the Lord.

JEREMIAH 30:17

Do you remember the last time
you got sick?

You felt terrible! God's Son Jesus
has been called the "Great Physician,"
or the great doctor. That's because you
can ask Jesus or God to help you feel better.
You can also ask God to be with your
doctors and nurses so that they will
know just what to do. God hears every
word you say to Him. God made you
and you are so precious to Him!

The Bible Promise Book for Preschoolers

If any of you lack wisdom, let him ask of God, that giveth to all men liberally.

JAMES 1:5

Do you know everything ?

No matter how much you learn there will always be something you don't know. If there is something you don't understand, ask God to help you. God said He will give you <u>wisdom</u>. God will help you to understand.

The Bible Promise Book for Preschoolers

Beloved, let us love
one another: for love is of
God; and every one that
loveth is born of God, and
knoweth God.

I JOHN 4:7

Where does love come from?

The Bible, God's special Book, says
that God is love. He has given you so
much love that you have plenty of extra
love. Where can love go? Anywhere.
You can share God's love with everyone
around you.

The Bible Promise Book for Preschoolers

We love Him, because He first loved us.

1 JOHN 4:19

How much does God love you?

God knew who you were before you were born. God loved you before you were born. God's love is greater than any other love. That's because no one — nothing — is greater than God.

The Bible Promise Book for Preschoolers

The Lord preserveth all them that love Him.

PSALM 145:20

Do you love God ?

Jesus told us to love God with all our heart, all our soul, and all our mind. That means you should love God with everything inside you. If you love God, God will always be with you.

And we know that all things work together for good to them that love God.

ROMANS 8:28

Do you love God all the time?

Sometimes bad things happen. You may spill paint on your new dress. You may fall down outside and scrape your knees. Your friend may not want to play with you. But you should never stop loving God. Even during bad times God loves you. God will always do what is best for you.

For Thou, Lord, wilt bless the righteous.

PSALM 5:12

When you love God do you act differently ?

The Bible says if you love God, you do what is right. God will take care of you. God wants to be the most important part of your life.

And they that know Thy name will put their trust in Thee: for Thou, Lord, hast not forsaken them that seek Thee.

PSALM 9:10

What does it mean to be a best friend?

A best friend is always there when you need them. Just as the sun comes up every day, God is always there. God is stronger than anyone or anything. God is everywhere and He knows everything. God wants to be with you every day. God wants to be your best friend.

And ye shall eat in plenty, and be satisfied, and praise the name of the Lord your God.

JOEL 2:26

Do you thank God for your food?

Before you eat you should close your eyes and bow your head and thank God for your food. God gives you so much to be thankful for. All of the wonderful things you have to eat come from God.

Behold the fowls of the air: for they sow not, neither do they reap, nor gather into barns; yet your Heavenly Father feedeth them. Are ye not much better than they?

MATTHEW 6:26

Who feeds the wild birds and animals?

You never see little sparrows going to the market to buy food. Or bears sitting in a restaurant having some breakfast. God feeds all of the wild birds and animals. But you are more important to God than all the animals. God will always take care of you.

The Bible Promise Book for Preschoolers

And he shall be like a tree planted by the rivers of water, that bringeth forth his fruit in his season.

PSALM 1:3

Have you ever picked an apple from a tree?

God is like a gardener and you are like a tree. God makes sure you have plenty of water and sunshine to help you grow. God wants you to "bloom" and tell others about Him.

The Lord is good, a strong hold in the day of trouble; and He knoweth them that trust in Him.

NAHUM 1:7

Have you ever seen a fire engine rushing to a fire?

Just like a fire engine with its sirens blaring and lights flashing, God is always ready to hurry to your side. There is no problem that is too big for Him. He is more powerful than anything or anyone in the universe. God is awesome!

The Bible Promise Book for Preschoolers

And ye shall seek Me,
and find Me, when ye shall
search for Me with all your
heart.

JEREMIAH 29:13

Do you play hide and seek ?

That's a fun game to play with your
friends and family. But God does not
play that game. God will never hide
from you. God is always there to help
you, listen to you, and most of all, to
love you.

The Bible Promise Book for Preschoolers

Blessed is that man that maketh the Lord his trust.

PSALM 40:4

Does the sun come up every morning?

That's God's way of saying, "Have a wonderful day!" You can trust God to always do what He says. You can trust God to always be there, morning, noon, and night.

In all thy ways acknowledge Him, and He shall direct thy paths.

PROVERBS 3:6

Have you ever tried to follow a map?

God is like a map. God will show you which way to go and what to do. Just ask Him to help you. Let God be your map.

Thy Word is a lamp unto my feet, and a light unto my path.

PSALM 119:105

Have you ever tried to find your way in the dark?

You probably bumped into furniture. Maybe you even fell down! When you don't know where you're going, or what to do, you can read God's special Book, the Bible. God will speak to you through His Words. God will keep you from falling down.

The Bible Promise Book for Preschoolers

All scripture is given by inspiration of God, and is profitable for doctrine, for reproof, for correction, for instruction in righteousness: That the man of God may be perfect.

2 TIMOTHY 3:16,17

Why is it important to follow directions ?

If you don't, you won't be able to finish a project. The Bible is a big book of important directions. If you follow God's directions, you will be happy your whole life.

The Bible Promise Book for Preschoolers

Thou shalt make thy prayer unto Him, and He shall hear thee.

JOB 22:27

Do you ever need to talk to God?

When you talk to God, you are <u>praying</u> to Him. God loves to hear your prayers! He is always there to listen to you. No matter where you are, God can hear you. You can ask God for help for yourself or someone else. You can thank God for His goodness and tell Him how much you love Him.

The Bible Promise Book for Preschoolers

Wait on the Lord: be of good courage, and He shall strengthen thine heart: wait, I say, on the Lord.

PSALM 27:14

Will God answer your prayers right away?

Not always. Sometimes God has a special reason to wait. He knows what will happen in the future. God knows the best time to answer your prayers. Wait for God to do things His way, the best way.

The Bible Promise Book for Preschoolers

For Thou art my hope, O Lord God: Thou art my trust from my youth.

PSALM 71:5

Have you ever been so sad you just can't get happy again?

Sometimes everything around you seems bad. When that happens you can tell God everything that is bothering you. You can pray. God will always hear you. God will always love you.

And she shall bring forth a son, and thou shalt call His name Jesus: for He shall save His people from their sins.

MATTHEW 1:21

Whose birthday do you celebrate at Christmas?

Jesus' birthday, the birthday of God's only Son! Long ago God's Son Jesus lived on the earth. He was put to death on a cross and was buried. Three days later Jesus came alive again! Jesus died and came alive again because He loves you. Jesus "paid the price" for everything bad you think or do. Because of Jesus, after you die you will live forever in heaven. Heaven is God's home.

God Has a Home

The Bible Promise Book for Preschoolers

And this is the record, that God hath given to us eternal life, and this life is in His Son.

I JOHN 5:11

What is eternal life ?

When you have eternal life you are able to live forever. If you believe that Jesus is God's Son, one day you will go to heaven. You will live in heaven eternally, forever. Even though no one knows exactly what heaven is like, we do know God's home is the most beautiful place you could imagine.

The Bible Promise Book for Preschoolers

Therefore if any man be in Christ, he is a new creature.

2 CORINTHIANS 5:17

Have you ever seen a butterfly come out of its coccoon?

Did you know that you are like a butterfly? When you say you believe in Jesus, you have become a new person. Now you will live your life to please God. Someday your earthly body will die. But, just like a butterfly, you will fly up to heaven. There you will live with God and all your family and friends who love God. Remember, God loves you forever!

And He took them up in His arms, put His hands upon them, and blessed them.

MARK 10:16